# Module 2 • Set 2 • Safety

## CONTENTS

This book belongs to

. . . . . . . . . . . . . . . . . .

Great Minds® is the creator of *Eureka Math*®, *Wit & Wisdom*®, *Alexandria Plan*™, and *PhD Science*™.

*Geodes*® are published by Great Minds in association with Wilson Language Training, publisher of Fundations®.

**Credits**

- *Super Spiny Mouse*: More page, photo by bogdanhoda/Shutterstock.com

- *Thorny Devil*: Special thanks to George Six for his guidance; front cover, Chris Watson/Shutterstock.com; title page, Rebecca Harrison/Shutterstock.com; p. 1, © Michael and Patricia Fogden/Minden Pictures; pp. 2–3, Kristian Bell/Shutterstock.com; pp. 4–5, John van Hasselt/Sygma/Getty Images; p. 6, Joslin Stevens/Shutterstock.com; p. 8, ronnybas/Shutterstock.com; p. 9, David South/Alamy Stock Photo; p. 10, imageBROKER/Alamy Stock Photo; p. 11, feathercollector/Shutterstock.com; pp. 12–13, Chris Watson/Shutterstock.com; p. 14, Avalon/Photoshot License/Alamy Stock Photo; More page, Bildagentur Zoonar GmbH/Shutterstock.com; back cover, mark higgins/Shutterstock.com.

- *The Crab and the Urchin*: More page, photo by Nature Picture Library/Alamy Stock Photo

- *Stick with Us*: folio icon, larryrains/Shutterstock.com; About the Animal Groups page (top), Rich Carey/Shutterstock.com, (middle), Piraneus/Shutterstock.com, (bottom), Lee Torrens/Shutterstock.com; More page, Design Pics Inc/Alamy Stock Photo

# Super Spiny Mouse

written by Emily Gula

illustrated by Sydney Hanson

A cat can hiss.

A crab can pinch.

A skunk can stink.

What can this mouse do
to stay safe?

He is small.
He fits in your hand.
He is a spiny mouse.

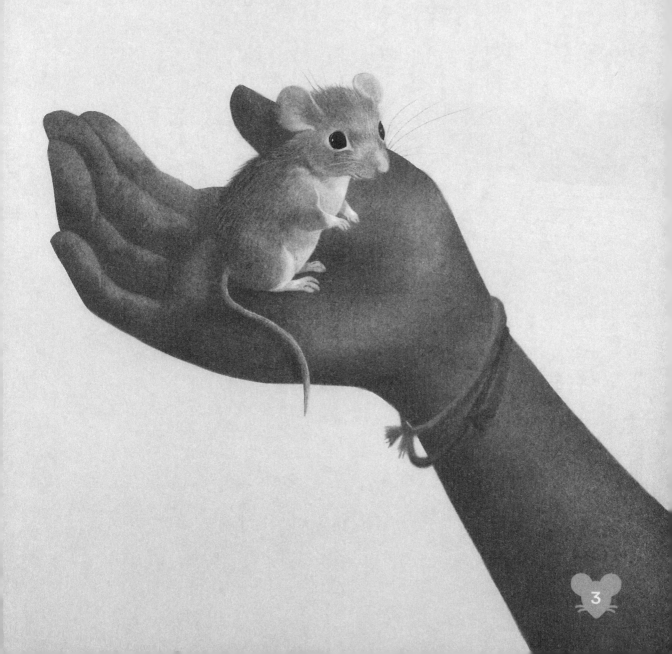

*Ssss, ssss, ssss . . .*
Here is a snake.
She hunts for lunch.

Is Spiny out of luck?

No!

His hair is too stiff
to munch.

She skips this snack.

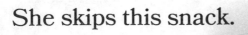

He is safe,

but not for long.

Flap, flap, flap . . .

Here is a hawk.

She grabs his tail.

Is Spiny out of luck?

No!

She snips his tail.

His tail pops off.

But he can still run.

He is safe,

but not for long.

*Shush, shush, shush . . .*

Here is an owl.

She plucks him up.

Is Spiny out of luck?

No!

She chomps a chunk.

He sheds

that patch of skin.

But his skin
will mend fast.

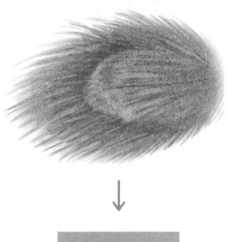

bare spot

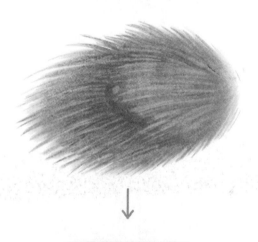

scab

new skin and hair

13

A snake can hunt.

A hawk can grab.

An owl can pluck.

What can this small mouse do?

He can stay safe!

# More

Some reptiles and amphibians can grow new body parts, but most mammals cannot. Two species of African spiny mice are the only mammals known to be able to regrow body tissue.

The skin of these spiny mice tears easily, but it also heals very quickly. In just one day, an injured spiny mouse can heal more than half its wound. Within three days, a spiny mouse covers its wound with new skin. Within three weeks, it can grow new hair. For some wounds, the spiny mouse can even regrow cartilage—a strong, flexible tissue found in body parts such as ears.

Scientists are intrigued by this speedy recovery. They study spiny mice to understand how these mice can heal so quickly. Scientists hope to apply their findings to improve healing in humans as well.

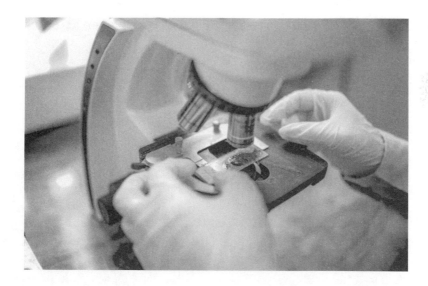

# Más

Algunos reptiles y anfibios pueden regenerar nuevas partes del cuerpo, pero la mayoría de los mamíferos no lo pueden hacer. Los únicos mamíferos que pueden regenerar tejido del cuerpo son dos especies de ratones espinosos africanos.

La piel de estos ratones espinosos se rompe con facilidad, pero también cicatriza rápidamente. En solo un día, un ratón espinoso lastimado puede curar más de la mitad de su herida. En tres días, el ratón espinoso cubre su herida con piel nueva.  En tres semanas, le puede crecer pelo nuevo. En algunas heridas, el ratón espinoso puede llegar a regenerar cartílago que es un tejido flexible y fuerte que se encuentra en partes del cuerpo como las orejas.

Los científicos están intrigados con esta capacidad de recuperarse rápidamente. Estudian a los ratones espinosos para comprender cómo pueden curarse tan rápido. Los científicos esperan poder aplicar sus hallazgos para también mejorar el proceso de curación en los seres humanos.

# THORNY DEVIL

by Marya Myers

The sun is up,
and it is hot.
A lizard spots his lunch.

This is a thorny devil.
He is small
and lives in the desert.
He has sharp spikes all over.

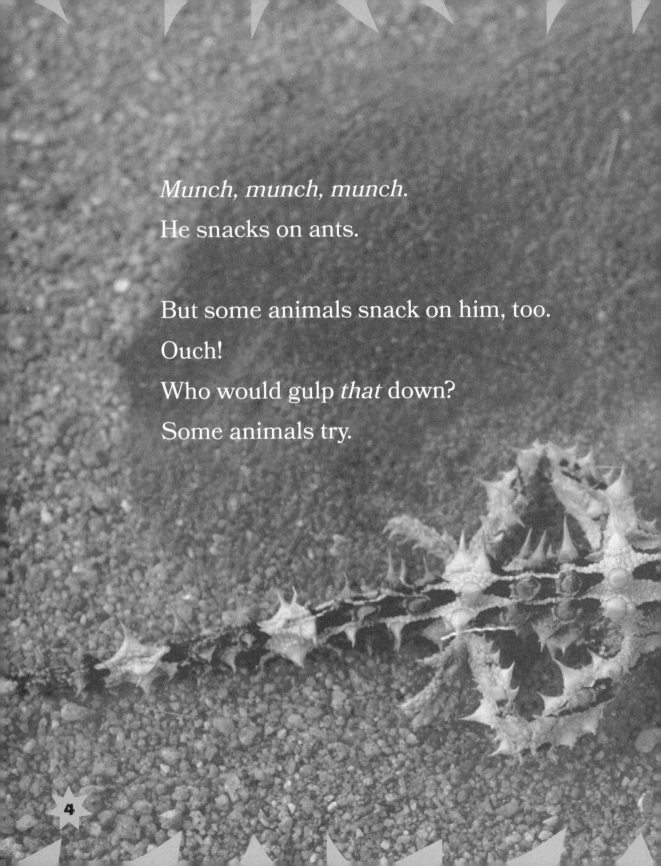

*Munch, munch, munch.*
He snacks on ants.

But some animals snack on him, too.
Ouch!
Who would gulp *that* down?
Some animals try.

4

What if an animal

picks him for lunch?

He will be safe.

He has tricks for that!

## COLOR SHIFT

In the hot sun,

he is tan and red.

He can hide well

in the red sand.

In the shade of a shrub,

he is black.

His skin shifts color

to help him be safe.

The bird does not see him!

# BIG CHEST

If the bird does spot him,

he has another trick.

He lifts his chest.

He puffs it up with air.

The bird thinks

*that* lunch is too big!

# TRICK HEAD

If a bird drops down on him,

he does his best trick yet.


He can drop his head to his legs.

Then, a fake head will pop up!

The bird can peck,

but he will be safe.

The sun sets.

The thorny devil is small.

He has tricks.

He will be safe for one more day.

# MORE

The thorny devil needs water to survive in the desert, but it does not use its tongue to drink. In the early morning, the lizard stands in damp patches of sand to soak up the moisture through its skin. The lizard also uses its tail to put the sand on its back to gather even more water.

The lizard's skin is designed to absorb water. It is covered with tiny grooves. The grooves act like straws to suck up any water the lizard's skin touches. Just as liquid spreads across a paper towel, water moves across the lizard's skin to reach its mouth.

# MÁS

El diablo espinoso necesita agua para sobrevivir en el desierto, pero no usa su lengua para beber. Temprano por la mañana, la lagartija se para en zonas de arena húmeda para absorber la humedad a través de su piel. La lagartija también utiliza su cola para colocar arena sobre su espalda y absorber aún más agua.

La piel de la lagartija está diseñada para absorber agua. Está cubierta de pequeños canales. Estos canales funcionan como pajillas que absorben el agua que toca la piel de la lagartija. Así como el líquido se extiende en papel absorbente, el agua se desplaza de la piel de la lagartija hasta la boca.

# The Crab
# and the
# Urchin

written by **Cate Oliver**

illustrated by **Lesley Vamos**

# Swish, swish.

In the sea,

grass tilts this way and that.

Ten thin legs brush past.

A crab is in a rush.

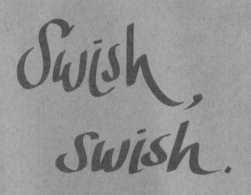

1

The sea is vast.
The crab is small.
Just two inches long.

Can this habitat be safe
for an animal like this?

# Flick! Flick!

The crab flicks his antennae.

What's that he whiffs?

3

A fish.

A big fish.

A big fish with big teeth!

4

# Gulp! Gulp!

The crab must act fast.

He digs and sinks into the sand.

Time to sit still.

*Hush, hush.*

The crab waits
until he thinks he is safe.
Then, he takes a risk.
Up pop his two eyes.

6

What's that he spots?

An urchin.

A sea urchin.

A sea urchin with sharp spines.

What luck!

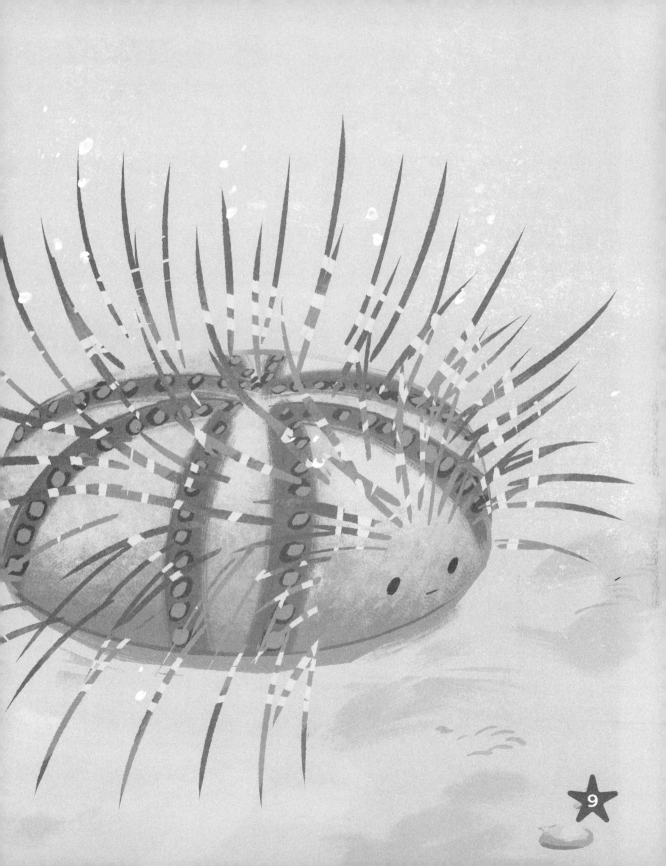

The crab grips the urchin
with his back legs.
Then, he puts her
onto his back.

# Zip! Zip!

The two are off in a flash.

Fish whiz by,
one by one.
Small fish.
Big fish.
Fish with spots.
Fish with stripes.
Lots and lots and lots of fish.

The urchin's spines mask the crab.

The fish do not see him.

He is safe at last.

13

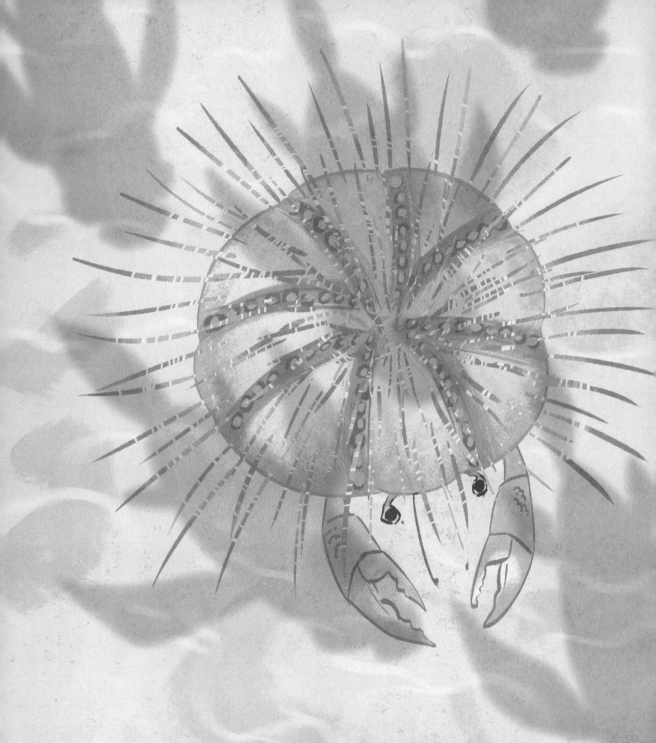

The crab and the urchin
trick them all.

14

# More

Crabs and sea urchins have special features that protect them from the dangers of the deep.

The crab has an outer shell, or exoskeleton. The hard shell protects it from predators. Fish cannot bite through the armor-like exoskeleton. A growing crab sheds, or molts, its exoskeleton. There is a soft new shell underneath. This new exoskeleton can take several weeks to harden.

Like the crab, the sea urchin has a special feature for defense. The sea urchin relies on its spines for defense. The urchin's spines poke attacking predators, such as sea stars. Some spines contain venom, a poisonous fluid. If the spines break, they regrow in a few days.

# Más

Los cangrejos y los erizos de mar tienen características especiales que los protegen de los peligros de las profundidades.

El cangrejo tiene un caparazón externo o exoesqueleto. El caparazón duro lo protege de los depredadores. Los peces no pueden morderlo porque su exoesqueleto funciona como una armadura. Un cangrejo en crecimiento muda o se desprende de su exoesqueleto. Debajo hay un nuevo caparazón suave. El endurecimiento de este nuevo exoesqueleto puede llegar a demorar varias semanas.

Al igual que el cangrejo, el erizo de mar tiene una característica especial de defensa. El erizo de mar cuenta con espinas para defenderse. Las espinas del erizo se clavan en los depredadores, como las estrellas de mar, que vienen a atacarlo. Estas espinas tienen veneno, un fluido tóxico. Si se rompen las espinas, se regeneran en pocos días.

# STICK WITH US

BY EMILY CLIMER · ILLUSTRATED BY JEN CORACE

In the sea,

we spin, we swish.

We swim as one—

a school of fish.

1

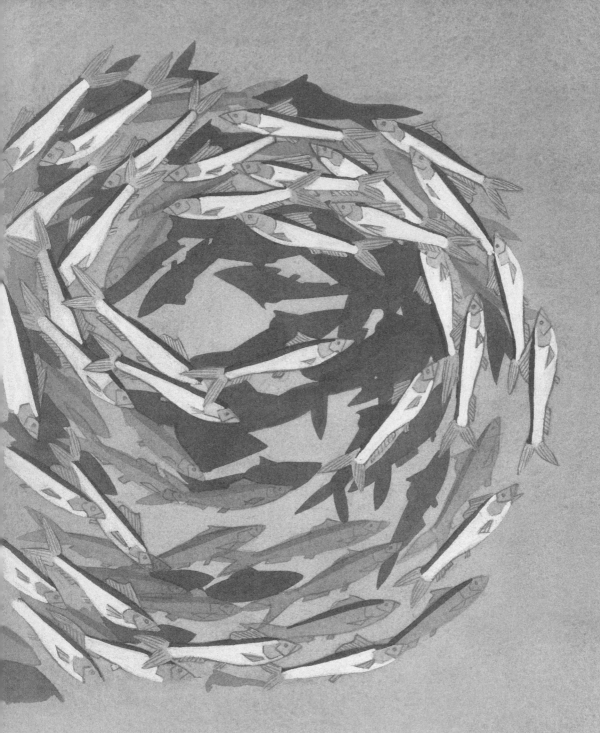

In our big group,

there is no gap . . .

. . . for hunting sharks

will snip and snap!

When this shark hears

the dinner bell,

we swish and swirl

to cast a spell.

4

We are no snack

to sit and munch!

Ask us the plan?

Stick in a bunch.

5

In the sky,
wing to wing—
we have no boss,
no rank, no king.

A flock of birds
has many eyes.
We spot a trap
and sing a cry!

Dip left, tilt right—
we flap with skill.
That hawk we spot
must want his fill.

8

A sudden dive—
then one quick shift.
The flock is safe.
Our group's a gift.

Here on the land,
we can't sit back.
We, too, must plot—
or be a snack.

A herd of sheep
can munch the grass
with much less fear
of what will pass.

11

When this red fox
runs for a hunt,
you do not wish
to stand up front.

12

In one big group,
we face the threat.
So stick with us—
it's your best bet!

13

# ABOUT THE ANIMAL GROUPS

## school of sardines

 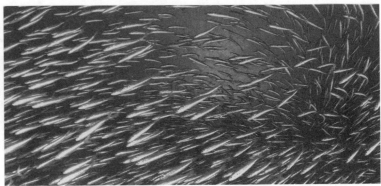

## flock of starlings

## herd of sheep

# MORE

Whether small worms or huge oxen, animals work together to protect themselves.

In the Amazon rainforest, scientists have observed sawfly larvae clustered on tree trunks. As a group, these small larvae look like a large flower. Each larva appears to be a single petal. Hungry predators are fooled by this wiggling flower arrangement.

Far to the north in the Arctic, herds of hulking musk oxen defend themselves from predators in two ways. If a lone wolf approaches, the oxen form a line. They prepare to charge. If a pack of wolves approaches, the oxen form a circle. Each musk ox faces outward, with its large horns ready to attack. Working together, the whole herd stays safe.

# MÁS

Los animales, ya sean pequeños gusanos o grandes bueyes, colaboran para protegerse.

En la selva amazónica, los científicos han observado las larvas de las moscas de sierra. En grupo, estas pequeñas larvas parecen grandes flores. Cada larva se parece a un pétalo. Con esta forma de organizarse, logran engañar a sus hambrientos depredadores.

Más al norte, en el Ártico, las manadas de bueyes almizcleros se defienden de los depredadores de dos formas. Si se aproxima un lobo solitario, los bueyes forman una línea y se preparan para atacar. Si se aproxima una manada de lobos, los bueyes forman un círculo. Cada buey mira hacia afuera, con sus largos cuernos listos para atacar. Al colaborar, se logra la seguridad de la manada.